FROM DOPE TO HOPE

Kim Kopal Perez

LIST OF CHAPTERS

Intervention / Praying Parents

One Wednesday evening in November of 2016, I was out at dinner when my phone rang. It was my mom.

"Hey Kimmy," she said warmly, "would you like to go to a women's getaway weekend? I have a friend here from church who has an extra ticket. I can't get off work, but the moment she offered it, I thought of you."

Immediately, I felt the familiar tension tighten in my chest. My fiancé had always struggled with control and jealousy, and the idea of me going away, especially without him, was something I knew could easily turn into a fight. Trying to diffuse the situation before it started, I casually hit the speakerphone button and said, "Hey… can you repeat that?"

She did. Every word now audible in the open space between us. He paused. Looked at me. Then nodded and said it was fine. He gave me permission to go and agreed that my sponsor could pick me up Friday morning.

It was settled. Just like that.

But deep down, I already knew - this weekend would be more than just a getaway. It would be the beginning of something I couldn't yet explain.

I was in trouble with the law again. This time because of an active meth addiction. I was living with an older man who had recently proposed. If I said yes, it would be my fourth marriage.

In my head, I had imagined the upcoming weekend as an escape - clubbing, partying, massages - a true getaway. A break from chaos. But that's not at all what happened.

The weekend was called Discovery Dallas, a three-day intensive self-help program developed by Dr. Phil and some of his colleagues. It was designed to help people confront their past, start healing, and walk away with a "contract" - a declaration of the person they truly wanted to become.

I packed for the weekend the way I always had before a binge: club clothes, a bottle of tequila, enough meth and cigarettes to last me three days. I had no idea that the weekend would change my life forever.

They asked us a question: What kind of woman do you want to be?

I stood up and said, "I am a woman of integrity and grace."

But the truth? I had zero integrity. My word meant nothing. I lied and manipulated constantly to get what I wanted. Yet something about saying it and declaring that vision of myself felt different.

Before the weekend ended, they told us this was only the first of three parts: Discovery 1 (the past), Discovery 2 (the present), and Discovery 3 (the future). Since I had gone in November, the next step -D2 - would be in January 2017.

Coming home from that weekend, I returned to the house of a man I barely knew. I was using him - a place to stay, someone to fund my addiction, while I stayed checked out on drugs.

Monday morning, I woke up groggy, completely drained from the intensity of the weekend. He shook me awake as I lay on the couch and told me I needed to pack my things and leave. He accused me of cheating on him, of stealing from him. He said I had taken his tools.

What happened next shocked both of us.

"I didn't steal your tools," I blurted out, "but I did sell your bullets."

The words fell out of my mouth before I could stop them. I remember thinking, Kim, why would you say that? But at that moment, I realized - I had just told the truth. For the first time in a very long time, I was honest. Without even meaning to.

I called my mom and asked her to come over and help me pack. She arrived, gathered my things, and took me straight to my sponsor's house.

When we got there, my sponsor looked at me and asked, "Kim, what kind of woman are you?"

Without hesitation, I said, "I am a woman of integrity and grace."

That weekend's declaration still echoed in my heart. And I believe with everything in me that God heard my cry.

Everything I owned fit into my SUV. My mom offered to let me come stay at her house. But the only thing on my mind was going to the bar. Because to me, alcohol was fun. Alcohol meant escape.

That night, I closed the bar like I always did. At 3 a.m., I sat alone in the parking lot. I had nowhere to go. No home. No plan.

And in that desperate, empty moment, I cried out:

God, if You're real, You've got to help me. You've got to do something.

And He did.

I felt Jesus in that car. I felt peace. I felt contentment.

I felt hope - something I had never known before.

I don't know if I passed out or was knocked out by His presence. But I woke up the next morning a completely different person.

Later, I called my dad. "I have Jesus in my heart," I told him.

He replied casually, "Yeah, of course you do."

I said, "No - you don't understand. I didn't before. I thought I did. But this feeling... this is like nothing I've ever experienced."

Did the old Kim change overnight? Of course not.

But I knew that I didn't want to be who I had been. I just didn't know what change looked like.

God did.

And He brought people into my life - my Discovery friends - who walked the journey with me.

From November to January, I gave up methamphetamine. But I still clung to alcohol, sex, and cigarettes.

At Discovery 2 in January, I made a commitment to give up alcohol. That was hard. I had been drinking daily since high school. I slipped a few times. But every single month, I allowed God to heal another broken part of me.

In February, during Discovery 3, I committed to not dating anyone for a full year. I wanted to give Jesus full access to my heart. I had to admit I was codependent. I used sex and seduction as survival. That year of surrender was the most healing thing I could have done.

For almost two years, I kept going back to Discovery every month. Sometimes to serve, sometimes just to sit in the lobby. Every conversation, every exercise, God used to heal parts of me I hadn't even known were broken. I became a woman of integrity. I gave up alcohol, casinos, sex outside of marriage, cussing, raunchy music, bars, and everything that had dragged me into self-destruction.

I started passing my drug tests. I completed my community service. I followed all my probation requirements. I stopped blaming others. I stopped playing the victim. I realized that my life was the result of my choices, and the only person responsible... was me. I began to love myself. I began to receive God's love for me.

It's true - His kindness leads us to repentance.

For so long, I called myself a Christian but lived in total rebellion - doing whatever I wanted, whenever I wanted. I spit in the face of the God I claimed to follow.

I started telling the truth. Owning my lies. Even the hard ones - abortion, lying about rape, stealing from people who loved me, carrying secrets I thought I'd take to the grave.

But the enemy only has power through secrets and lies. With every truth I spoke, the puppet strings were cut, and I stopped playing for the wrong team - the one that comes to kill, steal, and destroy.

Throughout my addiction, my parents never gave up on me. My mom always prayed for me, always spoke life over me. "You are a woman of God, and He loves you so much. He's got great plans for you."

I used to think, she doesn't even know me. If she did, she wouldn't say that. But the truth was: I didn't know me. I was the one trapped by lies.

My dad told me he prayed for me every day. I thought it was just something parents said. But now I know—the power of praying parents is real.

My mom's prayer? That God would send laborers into my life to share the good news. And He did.

My Discovery family, Denise Mailey, My TA Amanda, and even the woman from church, Pennie, who let me sleep on her couch. They were the laborers. They showed me the love of Jesus. They believed in me. They introduced me to true freedom through Christ and Discovery.

And my life has never been the same.

Childhood / Victim to Villain

I believe a lot of people assume trauma has to happen in childhood for someone to turn to drugs. But honestly, I grew up with caring parents who love the Lord. Nothing, in my eyes, was ever super traumatic.

Over the years, different people have tried to explain my story, offering theories like, "Maybe you've forgotten something," or "You weren't aware of what happened."

But here's what I know: Yes, I remember older girls kissing me or playing "house" with me as early as the age of four. I also have a memory of going down the street and getting a spanking from a neighbor, being told to pull my pants down.

I don't know what the motives of the adults around me or of the older kids were, but what I do remember is that as I got older, I began to enjoy playing house. I began to enjoy kissing girls.

We moved around a lot when I was a child. I always felt like a chameleon - adapting to wherever we lived.

When we lived out in the country, in Utopia, Texas, I wanted a pair of red lace-up cowboy boots. But when we moved to San Antonio, nobody wore cowboy stuff, so I dropped that desire fast.

That disease to please… the need to be liked and accepted… it always controlled me.

I never felt good enough. Never felt pretty enough. Never felt worth loving. I tried to earn affection and acceptance by blending in, buying things for people, and liking what they liked.

As I grew older, that stronghold led me into all kinds of trouble. Not just outward, physical trouble, but inward. My soul was hurting.

When we lived in Columbus, Texas, my parents worked at a camp. I remember stealing money just so I could go bowling with other fifth graders so I could buy them food and things.

In high school, I started playing sports. I began to thin out and, for the first time, I felt pretty. When guys started to notice me, it felt good. When they made advances, I didn't want to say no. I wanted them to like me.

I would steal CDs, makeup, clothes, or whatever I needed to keep up. I honestly don't know why. It felt like I had two lives.

One life - I was the pastor's daughter, an athlete, and a good student. Polite to all the parents.

The other life - I was an alpha female, I slept around, and I was cool. I did whatever I wanted.

I remember when my parents found out I was being promiscuous, my dad felt responsible. He questioned what they could have done differently. He questioned what he could've done to protect me from going down that path.

I'm not sure what I was thinking, but I wrote a letter saying I had been raped while visiting my grandmother in Las Vegas at the age of 12. In my 15-year-old mind, I thought I was protecting my dad. But now, as a parent, I can't believe I put him through that kind of torment - believing he hadn't protected his daughter.

I was selfish, and I was self-destructive. I got pregnant shortly after graduating from high school and gave up a volleyball scholarship to have my son. My mom praised me. She said I made the right choice, and that I was selfless. Later, when my son was three months old, I had an abortion of my second pregnancy. My excuse was that I didn't want to be a burden on my family - not after they had just stepped in to help me raise my first child.

The truth is, I had no idea who I was. And I didn't know who I wanted to be. I thought I was saved as a kid because I said the prayer of salvation, but honestly, now that I look back, I never gave Jesus the full access to my heart. I always chose the world. I always chose to be cool over everything else.

Abba / Santa Clause

The world places an immense amount of pressure on fathers and daughters and imposing expectations about what that relationship should look like.

I was fortunate enough to have a good father. He provided for me, and he made me feel loved. But the enemy, relentless in his pursuit, will use anything he can to create a gap and distance between us and the truth of what that relationship is meant to be. The world makes it nearly impossible to measure up to that ideal.

After I had my son, my parents got divorced. It was a devastating blow. My mom discovered my dad with her friend, embracing on the side of the road. There was so much division, accusations, and hazy, unclear narratives about what truly happened between them. But what I didn't realize then was that I too was a cheater. I lied, I slept around, and I did things I wasn't proud of, but I could never own up to them.

When you're a cheater, you assume everyone else is, too. When you're a liar, you believe others lie as well. We project onto others what we ourselves live out.

After my discovery experience, I began to truly know God as my Father. Growing up, I had a distorted view of God. I thought He was like Santa Clause. I imagined he had a list, made up of a naughty side and a nice side. Based on all the bad things I had done, I was sure I was on the naughty list.

I believed God didn't love me, and that He was angry with me. But then, after receiving Jesus into my heart, something changed. It was just like it's described in Ezekiel - the transformation of my heart from stone to flesh. I cried constantly, overwhelmed by the revelation of God's love, His kindness, and His goodness.

At the end of the day, I knew I could crawl into His lap, cry out with every ounce of my heart, and release all my pain.

There's a shift that happens in your heart when you truly come to know God as Abba.

In 2017, I went to Jesus Image in Houston, Texas. Kellie Copeland taught an afternoon session on ABBA. We were invited to come forward, to be prayed over and to receive the Father's love. I laid at the altar for hours, crying out all the hurt and all the pain I had carried for so long.

That afternoon, I was delivered from the Jezebel spirit - the girl who needed to show her body to get attention, the girl who slept around to feel loved, and the hurt girl who hurt others before they could hurt her. ABBA buried every pain with every tear that fell.

There's a song by Upper Room, called 'Father Song', sung by Elyssa Figueroa, and I would play it on repeat, over and over, for days on end, just soaking in the love of my Father in Heaven.

You were created by love, for love. Until you receive the love of your Father, your Creator, you will never fully allow anyone else to love you, not even your earthly family.

The truth is, it doesn't matter whether you had a good father or a bad father. It was never about that. It's about receiving the love of Abba Father. It's always been about receiving His love. Just like it says in John 3:16, "For God so loved the world that He gave His one and only Son, that whoever believes in Him shall not perish but have eternal life." That's love. The true love you've been searching for. The love that changes everything.

I think so many people struggle to receive the love of Abba Father because of the disappointment they've felt from their earthly fathers. Maybe they didn't even know their earthly father, and they have no concept of what a father is supposed to be, or what a father's love looks like, or what fatherly correction means. But here's the truth - a father's correction, a father's love, his endless laps where you can sit and cry and be held - that's what it's all about. And God is faithful. He created you. He loves you. He adores you. He loves your voice, the way you look, and the way you talk. He loves every detail because He designed it all.

I used to think the fear of the Lord meant being afraid of God, but I've come to realize it has nothing to do with fear at all. It's about honor. It's about honoring God so deeply that you would never do anything to hurt His heart. You would never choose anything or anyone over Him, His ways, or what He's asking of you.

There's a verse in the Bible that says, "If you're a friend of the world, you're an enemy of God." I spent nearly 36 years choosing the world over Him. But He never gave up on me, God was right there, waiting at the place of my surrender, ready to love me, hold me, and walk me through correction, direction, and protection. He is such a good Father.

He will not hold anything back from you. His ways are so much higher, so much better than anything we can imagine.

Let your Father love you. Let Him care for you and provide for you because that's what you were created for.

Prophecy / Recovery Homes

After Discovery, I spent the next two years chasing every move of God I could find including Upper Room worship and Todd White. I was hungry. My soul was desperate for something real. I remember standing in the sanctuary at Jesus Image in Houston in 2018 when Randy Needham gave me a prophetic word. He said I would one day help girls get off drugs - not from a place of brokenness, but from a place of healing. I didn't know at the time that the anointing on my life would be like honey - thick, slow, and passed down from the oil my parents carried. My first thought? "Oh no." That didn't sound like something I wanted to do. I didn't feel strong enough. Truthfully, I didn't feel like I could help people in addiction. But God had other plans.

Not long after that, I got another word. Brian Guerin stood up and said, "Someone in this room is going to find favor with the court system." I didn't think it was for me, until I returned home and was released early from probation in Wichita County. God's hand was already moving, even when I couldn't see it.

One day, a friend sent me a video of Todd White. Something about his message wrecked me. He said his mission was "to lead Christians to Christ," and it felt like he was talking about me. I had claimed the title "Christian" for years, but I had never really met Jesus.

It was at another Jesus Image gathering, when the Lord spoke clearly to my heart, that I was supposed to go to Todd White's school. I hadn't even gotten up from the altar yet, but I knew this was God, so right there in the sanctuary I gave my two weeks' notice for the temp agency where I had been working. I committed to following His call. Shortly after that, I saw a video of Todd White and Kenneth Copeland and it was complete confirmation.

I grew up going to the Kenneth Copeland conventions and those seeds of faith were planted in me. That is why I am so grounded in the word today. I heard it once said, "more is caught than taught." Before Jesus, it was just head knowledge and the word was never applied, but after Jesus, it was revelation. The word became Rhema - living and active in my life. When Todd and Brother Copeland did the video for the school it was introduced as a three-month intensive. So that fall, I moved to Dallas to attend Lifestyle Christianity University. I also applied for Upper Room Kids and was hired to work there with some amazing people. I watched God miraculously provide for every single need. For instance, one afternoon as I was fundraising by mowing yards, I broke my weed eater. I threw it down and said, "God, what now?" - that same evening a guy from our church knocked on our door and gave me a brand-new weed eater. God did that all throughout my journey. Every time I cried out, He answered.

In 2019, I was planning to graduate. But Todd announced an extension to the program. I didn't feel led to stay, and I didn't have the money, so I prayed. Instead, I began volunteering every Monday night at Hope Center Ministries in Wichita Falls. I'd drive up from Dallas, pick up a girl, spend the evening sharing the love of Jesus, and then drive back. Christi Goin, the Recovery Coordinator, saw something in me. One day she called and said, "There's an open position as Director. You should apply."

Exactly one year to the day from that original prophetic word, I was hired as Director of Hope Center in Holliday, Texas.

Hope Center, like any recovery program, isn't perfect. The women come in raw, broken, and often with entire families lost to addiction. I saw women who had children taken away by CPS continue to get pregnant, hoping one baby might fill the hole inside them. But unhealthy people create unhealthy patterns, and only Jesus can break that cycle.

The program itself was one year long. The first 30 days focused on bookwork and Celebrate Recovery curriculum. At 45 days, the women started working in local factories, learning how to "adult" again. It was a great opportunity for transition, but the environment wasn't always healthy. The man directly over me resisted the Holy Spirit and openly criticized leaders I admired. It was religion cloaked in control. After two years, they let me go. They said they'd had enough of "that Todd White stuff." But by then, the seeds had been sown. I had lived it, I had loved them through a growing season, and I had learned all I needed.

I believe with my whole heart that when someone is truly ready to get clean, they can do it anywhere. I never lived in a recovery home. I never walked through a 12-step program. My recovery home was a weekend away at the Discovery course and Jesus. That was enough.

Looking back, real recovery starts with truth. For years, I played the victim. I expected others to carry my weight, buy my cigarettes, pay my probation, and clean up my messes. But when I started facing the mirror, asking for forgiveness, and owning my choices, that's when integrity took root. That's when my words began to matter.

At Discovery, there's a tool we use. You can either live by your *poem* or live by your *contract*. The poem is how others experienced you at your worst.

My poem was:
Lost – Pretender – Scared – Alone – Manipulating – Wounded - Broken Soul

But my contract is:
My new identity declares that *I am a woman of integrity and grace.*

That to me is the definition of recovery. It is accepting what Jesus did on the cross and stepping into a brand-new life. The old is gone and I am forgiven. I am chosen, I am worthy, I am responsible, and my actions today will determine my outcome tomorrow.

Recovery isn't just detoxing your body. I believe it's renewing your mind. For the first couple of years, it's work

- hard work. But once you encounter real freedom, you're no longer "in recovery."

You are recovered! People will try to tell you that you'll always struggle, that you'll always have to fight, that you'll always be one drink or hit away, but that's the mindset of the world. The Kingdom says: *You're a new creation. Raised with Christ. Free indeed.*

One encounter with Jesus changes everything. He changed my taste buds. He changed my desires. I began feeling like I was on camera all the time - like the movie, The Truman Show. You can't hide and manipulate when everything you do is out in the open. I was constantly thinking, "This is being recorded. I need to tell the truth." I learned how to be honest about how I was feeling, what I was doing, and the thoughts I had. Because for years, I had buried my emotions and lied about everything. But real recovery feels like being in a room full of every person you've ever met, and now you have to tell your life story in front of them. You might as well tell the truth. The lies you tell don't just hurt them - they hurt you. And the truth?
The truth really does set you free.

Before Jesus, I danced for the devil at the front of the bar, beer bottle in hand. But now I dance for the King of Kings, and I am *unashamed.*

I love to say it this way, "There is no high like the Most High."

His blood is still enough.

Jesus / My Husband

In 2017, I gave Jesus a year.
No dating.
No kissing.
No holding hands.
Nothing.

That spring, I found myself at an ex's house, and I told him about the commitment I had made to not have sex. That same evening, after a few drinks, I fell asleep on his couch. I woke up to him making a move. Old Kim would've given in because for me, sex and alcohol always went together. But something had changed. For the first time since high school, I didn't feel pressured to care about how a man felt more than how I felt. I didn't feel the need to protect him from rejection. I didn't care what he thought about me anymore. That was freedom. I got up, got in my car, and I left.

During that season, when Jesus was the only man I turned to, my song of choice was "Clean" by Natalie Grant:

I see shattered
You see whole
I see broken
But You see beautiful
And You're helping me to believe
You're restoring me piece by piece

There's nothing too dirty

That You can't make worthy
You wash me in mercy
I am clean
There's nothing too dirty
That You can't make worthy
You wash me in mercy
I am clean

What was dead now lives again
My heart's beating, beating inside my chest
Oh I'm coming alive with joy and destiny
Cause You're restoring me piece by piece

There's nothing too dirty
That You can't make worthy
You wash me in mercy
I am clean
There's nothing too dirty
That You can't make worthy
You wash me in mercy
I am clean

Washed in the blood of Your sacrifice
Your blood flowed red and made me white
My dirty rags are purified
I am clean

Washed in the blood of Your sacrifice
Your blood flowed red and made me white
My dirty rags are purified
I'm clean, I'm clean

Washed in the blood of Your sacrifice
Your blood flowed red and made me white
My dirty rags are purified
I'm clean
I am clean
I'm clean
Oh You made me
You wash me
Clean
Oh You made me clean

In Discovery 3, you're given a mission. My first mission was this: *To help brokenhearted women find freedom through telling my story.*

And after surrendering my codependency, this became my declaration: *My name is Kim. I am a woman of integrity and grace. My mission is to empower others by tearing down the lies of the enemy and letting them know that their self-worth and validation doesn't come from a person, a place, or a thing. Your self-worth comes from within, from knowing Jesus.*

This revelation of Jesus as Comforter… as Best Friend… as Boyfriend… has been the well that never runs dry. Everything I was ever looking for I found in Him. I had spent so long trying to find the man who would love me for me. For 36 years, I chased that.
But all the while, I didn't even know who I was. I didn't know what I liked, or didn't like. I was so hurt, so broken, and I chose men out of convenience and alcohol.

Three times I've been married.
The first was Eric. An African American man who spoke French. I met him at a bar in Dallas when my son Cameron was just a baby. I cheated on him over and over. I used him as a babysitter... until I finally left him for another man.

The second marriage was Orlando. A Hispanic man I met at a country bar in Wichita Falls, Texas. That was probably my most toxic relationship. He was actively in addiction and struggled with mental illness. He was the reason I got arrested for the first time in Wichita Falls. He purposely smashed his head on the side of the house and said that I had attacked him. The charges were dropped, but I'll never forget the feeling of going back to him and me believing that being treated like that was all I deserved.

The third marriage was to a White man named Brad. I believe we had a genuine relationship. We loved each other, but we loved alcohol more. And without God at the center, no relationship can survive.

I had set aside one year for Jesus to be my husband. But that year turned into four and a half - and I loved every moment of being romanced by Jesus. I even had date nights, lit candles, and imagined Him sitting across the table from me. We had long conversations after hard days and romantic walks.

That season of being single, honestly, didn't even feel like I was single. Because Jesus was healing me - healing my need for approval, my need for attention, and my need for false security. He heals everything, He restores all things, and Jesus truly did it in my life.

He turned me from dirty to clean. Years of feeling stained and worthless were washed white as snow. When I got baptized, I truly died with Him. And I rose with Him to be created new. Like a virgin - I had a brand-new start. It's the best feeling in the world. Before Jesus, I never let myself stay single for long. There were always guys I could call to feel better or sleep around with. I called them my backup plans. But after surrendering, after truly letting Jesus be Lord of my life - I wouldn't even entertain conversations that crossed the line. I wouldn't put myself in a position to be the old Kim. That girl, the one who needed validation from men, she's dead.

I became a woman of integrity and grace. I was content staying single, and letting Jesus be my husband until I met the man that God had for me.

The world offers the counterfeit.
But God... God is the real.
Never settle for the counterfeit. Wait for the real.
It is worth the wait.

Marriage / Disappointment & Destiny

The idea of being married again once felt so foreign to me. For years, Jesus had been my husband, my provider, my comforter, and my companion. But in Habakkuk 2:2, the Word tells us to *"write the vision and make it plain,"* and so I did. With a surrendered heart, I made a list. It was a simple, raw, and honest list of the kind of man I desired. I wanted a man who loved Jesus, who was unashamed and passionate in his worship. I desired that he would be a laid-down lover of the King. I wanted someone bold, attractive, covered in tattoos - yes, I know that doesn't sound traditionally "Christian," but I'm just being real. Most of all, I wanted someone I knew I wouldn't cheat on, because in every relationship before Jesus, I had been unfaithful. I wanted a man who wasn't just a Sunday believer, but someone who lived the Word, who actively walked by faith, and who carried the heart for ministry. When I think back to how Armando and I came together, there's no doubt—it was a *God story.*

Technically, we had known each other since junior high. His mom had attended the church where my parents pastored, and we even went to youth camp together one summer. Years later, I saw him again in high school. Then, many years later after that, in Bible College he was my small group leader. At that time, he was married. But, in the spring of 2020, he reached out to ask for prayer and let me know he had gone through a divorce. I assumed he had messaged our entire small group.

Fast-forward to May 2021 - my mom and I visited Lifestyle Christianity, and while we were there, I ran into someone from that same small group, a guy named Mikel who was now working with Todd White. He asked if I'd heard about Armando. I was hesitant to respond. I didn't want to gossip or mention his divorce, but Mikel wasn't talking about that. He said Armando had prayed over a blind girl and her eyesight had been restored. We both just stopped and praised God - Jesus the Healer was still moving.

Just a few weeks later, I was facing a challenging situation at church and didn't know who to turn to. Everyone I normally leaned on was either my boss at Hope Center Recovery Homes or my pastor. I needed wise, outside counsel, so I reached out to Armando. He prayed with me, listened, and showed genuine care. I told him about the plans I had with my friend, Audra. We had just started *Daughter of the King,* a women's home. I had recently formed an LLC, and he offered to help. He said he had a Zoom account and offered to host a call to encourage us and the team. That Friday, we gathered online - Kennedy, Erika, Audra, my mom, Jackie Sue, and Armando. He prayed and prophesied over every single one of us. And he was spot on. After we ended the call, my mom turned to her friend and said, *"I think I just met my son-in-law."*

I didn't know it then, but a few months later at Randy Clark's Global Awakening event in Oklahoma City, the

Lord confirmed it. By October of that year, Armando and I were married.

The first time I saw him again in person since Bible School, the Holy Spirit whispered to my heart, *"You're going to bring him credibility."* Looking back, that word was weighty. He wasn't fully surrendered to God because of the trauma he had experienced in his divorce. His words were right, but his actions still wrestled with old patterns he had fallen back into. He had an ankle monitor, child support and financial debt, was on probation, and had relapsed into being a closet alcoholic. Unemployment hung over us for the first months of marriage. It wasn't easy. There was a lot to work through. Then came the moment that nearly broke me. He called me from Dallas, and the slur in his voice said everything. He had been drinking. That familiar ache from my past came rushing back. I had spent over half my life numbing my pain with alcohol. My instinct was to run. But I called my brother Chad first, and that phone call shifted everything.

He said, *"Kimmy, you've been working with people in addiction for the last two years. Don't you think God knew you'd be the one to help your husband? You can't just run. You have to break the curse of divorce in our family."*

After that call, I felt the Holy Spirit urge me to reach out to Angie at Hope Center. Pride had to die at that moment. I dropped my husband off at rehab and laid it all at the feet of Jesus. And oh, how God moved. In those 45 days, I watched a man transform. Armando began to own his mistakes, stop playing the victim, and make amends with the people he had hurt. He finally stepped into full surrender. And today? He is a man of honor, humility, and integrity - truly walking in his calling.

You can only go as far as your character will carry you. And now, God knows He can trust us. We don't just preach it, we *live* it. We're not one way in public and another behind closed doors. From sunrise to sunset, we live for Jesus. There's no yelling. No cussing. No chaos. That old life is buried. That brokenness is healed. That desire for worldly approval is gone. We are sold out - body, soul, and spirit - to the Father, Son, and Holy Ghost.

Armando blessed me with three beautiful bonus children - Paige, Noah, and Drake and together with my greatest gift, my son Cameron, we are a family of five. God has restored everything the enemy tried to steal. What I once saw as a disappointment turned out to be *destiny*. Of course, I made mistakes along the way. I didn't choose God quickly. But when did I do it, I chose Him with everything I had. God knew that once I said yes, I'd never go back. I spent so long playing for the wrong team - living as a confessing Christian with no real relationship with Christ. But after 2016, when I encountered the living God, everything changed. I know without a doubt, if I had died before then, I wouldn't have made it to Heaven. I was a friend of the world, and James 4:4 says whoever is a friend of the world is an enemy of God. But God, in His mercy, rescued me. He redeemed me. And now, I'm living proof of what grace can do.

I won't pretend. I won't perform. I'm not interested in polished religion. I am here to be real, raw, and authentic because that's where the power is. And though I wasn't always there for my son through his early years, God has restored that too. I can parent with purpose, love my children well, and speak the truth with confidence. Because only *truth* sets us free. The call on my life is irrevocable. God knew every detail before I was born. And I wouldn't change one thing about my past - it made me who I am today.

"For I know the plans I have for you," declares the Lord, "plans to prosper you and not to harm you, plans to give you a hope and a future." - Jeremiah 29:11

Hard seasons aren't punishment, they're preparation. Growth is born in discomfort. And comfort? That comes only from the Comforter Himself.

After three marriages without Jesus, God gave me a husband who is my best friend, my partner in ministry, and the father I never thought my children would have. He is every detail of that list I wrote down, and so much more. He's a man who adjusts when corrected, he forgives quickly, and he listens to God. My mom always says, *"Pride makes excuses. Humility makes adjustments."* My husband is a humble man who makes adjustments daily to walk in step with the Holy Spirit. Like Paul said, *"Follow me as I follow Christ."* And I get to do just that. I submit to my husband because I trust the One he's following.

Our mission is simple: to bring revival to every city and nation with the life changing power of Jesus Christ. I am a woman of integrity and grace. He is fearless and full of faith. And together - we are proof that God can redeem *anything.*

Holy Spirit / Healings

One thing that was deeply instilled in me from childhood was the power and presence of the Holy Spirit as our Helper. I can still hear my mom's voice anytime I lost something - "Ask the Holy Spirit; He knows where it is." That was always her answer. Whether it was a lost book, a favorite shirt, or an answer to a question, she would point me to Him: Holy Spirit—our Comforter, Counselor, and constant guide.

Now, as I've grown older and deeper in my walk with Jesus, I've come to realize that being Spirit-led is one of the greatest treasures of our faith. It's not always about big, dramatic encounters. Sometimes, it's as simple as a Band-Aid. I remember being in a Dollar Tree Store one day when I felt a gentle nudge from the Holy Spirit, "Get those Band-Aids." I didn't need them, and I rarely use Band-Aids, but I obeyed. Just hours later, while I was at work at the law office, a woman from upstairs walked in asking if we had any Band-Aids because she had cut her finger. I smiled and handed them to her. "The Holy Spirit knew you needed these," I told her.

That's the beauty of being led by the Spirit. It might seem small in the moment, but it has an eternal impact. He'll prompt you to grab something, speak to someone, turn around, or pray, and though it may feel inconvenient or confusing at first, obedience to those whispers brings supernatural fruit. Your one act of obedience could be the answer to someone else's heart cry.

I'll never forget the time Armando and I were leaving the grocery store, and he felt the prompting to pray for a woman and her young granddaughter. As he prayed, the woman broke down in tears. Her husband had recently passed, and she was drowning in grief. I truly believe she was on the edge of giving up completely. That moment wasn't about religion; it was about rescue. The Holy Spirit had orchestrated that encounter, and her life was touched because someone listened.

Jesus Himself said, "It is better that I go away so that the Helper may come." Yet so many believers walk around not accessing the very Spirit Jesus gave His life to send us. Churches get caught in schedules and agendas, rushing past the moments when the Spirit wants to pour out healing, prophecy, and restoration. But the Holy Spirit isn't just here for goosebumps and Sunday services. He is here to partner with us every day. He wants to lead us into the miraculous and the practical, into healing both physical and emotional, just as 3 John 1:2 says: *"Beloved, I pray that you may prosper in all things and be in health, just as your soul prospers."*

Healing was something I saw all throughout my childhood. My own grandmother got out of a wheelchair at John Osteen's church in Houston. My sister was diagnosed with leukemia, and after prayer, it vanished. As a kid, I'd watch Benny Hinn's *This Is Your Day* and marvel as miracles unfolded. The presence of God was so real, so active. I always knew I could call my mom when I needed prayer. Her prayers carried weight. When she prayed, things shifted. But it wasn't until I had my own radical salvation in 2016, stirred by Todd White's outreach videos, that I realized I wanted to step out too. I didn't want to just watch others. I wanted to partner with the Holy Spirit to bring healing to the hurting. I attended Lifestyle Christianity's very first school semester and saw wonders like legs growing out, feathers falling, and gold dust appearing. But even then, I struggled to believe it could happen through me. I thought healing belonged to "the anointed." I felt that I wasn't gifted in that way, but I was wrong.

When Armando and I got married, he walked boldly in the healing power of Jesus. He once prayed for a blind girl, and her eyesight was fully restored. I saw scars disappear on people as he would pray. In those early months, almost every person he prayed for was instantly healed. But over time, I began to realize that it wasn't just him, it was Jesus. It was the Holy Spirit, and I had access to that same power. We don't need a special title. We need boldness and obedience.

Over this last year, I've seen people healed through my own prayers for back pain, legs growing out, headaches going away, and having them test their bodies. I used to think there was a "healing anointing," but now I understand that it's not about special gifting, it's about activation of the anointing inside of you. The same Spirit who raised Jesus from the dead lives inside of every believer. Even before I understood it, I had seen healing in my own body. I remember weed-eating one day when the line hit my toe. It started to bleed and swell, but as I began praying in tongues, the bleeding stopped, the swelling reversed, and it healed right there in front of my eyes. Another time at the gym, I hit my leg hard. I immediately took authority over it, laid hands, and watched the bruise and pain vanish. But in 2025, something shifted. I began stepping out with boldness, approaching people in public, asking if I could pray, and watching Jesus heal right then and there.

Here's how I usually pray:

- "From 0 to 10, what's your pain level right now?"

- "Do you believe Jesus can heal you right now?"

- Then I pray something like: "Father, I thank You that You are Healer. In Jesus' name, I command this pain to leave. I speak to this (body part) and declare healing by the finished work of the cross. Exodus 15:26 says, You are Jehovah Rapha—the God who heals."

Then I ask, "What do you feel? Is there any change?"

If there's only improvement, I pray again, boldly: "God, You're not a 50% healer. You're not 80%. You're 100%. I thank You for complete healing in Jesus' name."

When they get healed, we celebrate every miracle, big or small, because Jesus is glorified. Then I will pray directly over them and their future, and prophesy that God is going to do an amazing thing in their life.

Friend, let me tell you, **you** can be activated. You already carry the Spirit of God inside you. Don't wait for a stage, a microphone, or a ministry card. You have the Helper. Let

Him help you help others. Jesus is still healing. He's still saving. He's still moving. Don't be afraid to step out. Your simple yes might be someone's miracle. So go, pray, love, speak, and watch what God will do!

Total Immersion / Faith Generals

Have you ever found yourself in a place with God where He asks you to do something that makes absolutely no sense in the natural? Something like quitting your job or leaving an organization you thought you'd be with forever?

That's exactly what happened to me in December 2024. But really, the shift began a month earlier, when we attended an all-night prayer meeting in Kansas. At the altar that night, something shifted. I felt it. The glory realm opened, and when I got up off that floor, I was not the same. Something eternal had been deposited inside of me.

I had been previously working in the legal field for nearly four years. I loved my job, especially working for Mr. David Phillips, a man of integrity who truly honored justice. The law firm under his leadership felt righteous. We were doing good for people. But in March 2024, everything changed. Mr. Phillips passed away. I remember the moment clearly. I was at lunch when suddenly my ears clogged, and that's always been a sign to me that angelic activity is near. Later that evening, his wife called to share the news, and I knew right away what that sign had meant. The angels were rejoicing as they welcomed him home, celebrating his life of impact and honor.

After his passing, I began working for a different attorney. One who didn't operate in the same spirit of integrity.

Honestly, I don't think she was a believer. The atmosphere of my workplace wasn't the same. And after experiencing the glory of God so powerfully in Kansas, coming back to that environment felt unbearable. I found myself acting out of character, grieved in my spirit. I kept hearing the Lord whisper, "Kim, this is no longer the place for you." But I continued to wrestle.

"God, I made a commitment. This job pays well. She lets me take time off for ministry without complaint."

It didn't make sense to leave, and yet, I could feel the Holy Spirit urging me to trust Him with the next step. He was calling me out, but I was still clinging to my comfort.

A few weeks later, we attended Kings Church in Dallas, Texas and Dr. David Remedios released a prophetic word over me. He said something that struck deep: "God wants to know if you'll trust Him when you can't track Him." That word floored me. I fell out under the power of the Spirit and remained there for the entire service. To me, it felt like only a few seconds but that's how the glory realm works. It's like time ceases to exist and hours go by so fast. As I came to, I heard the woman holding the microphone declare, "God is your boss now."

I knew the Lord was confirming what He had already been saying. That happened in December, and still, I resisted. I told myself, "Just get past the holidays. Work isn't that bad." But the truth was, I was delaying obedience.

Then came Valentine's Day, 2025. The Lord whispered to my heart, "Will you let Me be your first love?" That was it. I wrote my resignation letter and turned it in. I let that day mark the beginning of a new journey - one of total immersion into the presence of God. A walk of radical trust, faith, and dependence on the Holy Spirit. And you know what? God has provided in every detail since.

Even though our expenses were higher as our ministry started to grow, God supplied every need. Miraculously, without my salary, He provided funds for our El Salvador missions and to purchase the tent my husband had felt led to buy for revivals. He sent people - not just financial supporters, but laborers. intercessors, and team members. He connected us with two on-fire evangelists we met on the Gospel crusade fields - Eric Crowley and Sean Wernsman. He linked us with revival pastors from Kansas. He even stirred the heart of an administrative powerhouse, Melissa Lang, who brought her disciple and joined our team. It was supernatural.

People from our church joined the movement - like Heidi and Kurt Robinson, who helped lead outreach during one of our revival weekends and witnessed 68 salvations in just two days. The Messmer's who made a way to bring KCBC students for outreach training. The Keener family shared Jesus with a young boy on a bicycle and that very day, the boy was baptized, filled with the Holy Spirit, and received his prayer language. He was nine years old.

This season of total immersion changed everything. We now have a ministry headquarters and each morning I get to walk into our prayer room and ask, "Holy Spirit, what do You want from me today?" Whether it's painting a room, making a balloon arch, running promotions for businesses, cleaning, or picking up kids from school, it's all worship. It's all obedience. Every gift God placed in me; He is now using. And He is bringing provision with it. This lifestyle is a laid-down life of obedience and intimacy and is worth everything I gave up.

The five tent revivals we've hosted so far have been powerful. The second one, originally planned for South Carolina, was supposed to be with the same recovery home network called Hope Center that I had been released from. Remember them thinking I was too radical? Here we were years later, and they pulled out of their commitment at the last minute. It was because I boldly challenged their spiritual leadership motives after I found out they despised teachings from Kenneth Copeland, Joel Osteen, and Steven Furtick. So instead of South Carolina, we hosted that tent revival in Texas. Perfect! After all, Texas is the revival capital of the world.

God has continued to move. Just like Romans 8:28 says, He works all things together for the good of those who love Him and are called according to His purpose. Every rejection, every disappointment, and every detour - He's used it to accelerate our calling.

But you know what? Growth never comes without discomfort. You only grow when you stretch. That's what this has been - it's a Holy Spirit stretch. And I've learned to recognize it. Now, when I feel stretched, I know something good is coming on the other side.

It's just like working out. My husband and I go to the gym every morning at 5 a.m. I started lifting 8-pound weights, and now I'm up to 20. It's progression, consistency, and discipline - that's exactly how it works with the Lord. You have to be willing to say, "I will trust You, even when I can't track You." I'll go against the flow. I'll do what doesn't make sense. I'll live my life laid down. I fear nothing but You, Lord, because You are with me.

This season has taught me that faith and immersion go hand in hand. Faith comes by hearing, and I needed to hear the Word daily. In those early weeks, I immersed myself in the teachings of Kenneth Hagin - learning how he stood on healing when others doubted it was for today. Then came John Osteen. I didn't even realize the impact he'd had on me. My parents took us to Lakewood Church during those years, and even as a child, the seeds he planted stayed in my spirit.

I heard it once said that more is caught than taught. Looking back, I remember He would hold up his Bible and say: "This is my Bible. I am what it says I am. I can have what it says I can have. I can do what it says I can do." That never left me. It had just been lying dormant until now. This season of immersion reawakened the voices of faith in my life and allowed me to go back and learn from those that have gone before us. There is literally a cloud of witnesses watching us and cheering us on from heaven. Oral Roberts used to say, "If you think this is something, just wait until the end-time Great Awakening." And I truly believe this is it. This is revival being born out of obedience with a heart for the harvest, to share the gospel and see the signs and wonders of God.

Kenneth Copeland conventions are something we always went to. It was a place we went to build up our faith. I didn't have to unlearn anything because my parents raised me in the Word of Faith. I was introduced to Kenneth and Gloria Copeland, Jesse Duplantis, Jerry Savelle, R.W. Schambach, and Hilton Sutton. These are Word of Faith generals. They taught the Bible, they believed it, and they lived it. They got a hold of the revelation that the bible isn't a manual of things not to do, but rather it is a high-performance manual, and if we implement what's in it, we will have a high-performance life.

God wants us to prosper and be in good health. He wants us to know that we're on the victory side and that every day is our receiving day. Every day we are called to tell people about Jesus. He also wants us to pray for people, lay hands on this sick, and watch them recover. There are no days off just like the gym. There is no at home Christian versus at Church Christian. This life is for Jesus in everything that we do.

Evangelist / Missionary Heidi Baker is one of my favorite examples, she lives and breathes for Jesus. One thing I have grown to know about the Faith generals or anyone that people come against – is that the devil hates truth and he will do whatever he can to keep the truth from you. That's why the world wants you to dislike these power evangelists and these faith filled generals. The enemy wants you to question prosperity when it comes to following Jesus. There's no such thing as a "prosperity gospel." There's the Gospel, and the Gospel is prosperous.

God wants us to live in victory. To walk in healing. To prosper and be in health as our souls prosper. The Word of Faith believes the bible, and it puts the bible to action. Today, we attend Eagle Mountain Church in Newark, Texas. This is the church founded by Kenneth Copeland, now led by Pastors George and Terri Pearsons. They never ask for money. They simply preach the Word. And when you grab hold of truth, you'll experience real revelation of generosity and sowing.

I want to encourage you to go back and listen to our forefathers. These faith generals who have gone before us, and those who are activated in the living word of God.

Here is a list - *Nancy Dufresne, Kenneth Copeland, Jesse Duplantis, Andrew Womack, Dan Mohler, Bill Johnson, Todd White, Jonathan Shuttlesworth, Ben Fitzgerald, Michael Koulianos, Randy Needham, Michael Miller, and Nathan Morris.*

We partner with Nathan Morris and get to go on the Crusade fields with Shake the Nations Ministries. We partner with those who are living out the great commission of Jesus. We also partner monetarily with Jesus Image, Kenneth Copeland Ministries, Louisiana Outpouring, - Dr. David Remedios, and CFAN/ Daniel Kolenda.

Recently I've been listening to Rodney Howard Brown. He's a fire evangelist too. And of course, Armando Perez.

Every time I listen to my husband it is a new download of what the Holy Spirit is saying to him. It's always new. It's always a fresh revelation. It'll set a fire deep in your soul.

It is important and 100% vital that you feed on the word of God daily. Don't expect your pastor to give you everything you need once a week. Open your Bible and eat the Word.

John Bevere once said: "Every morning when I wake up, I don't eat natural food until I've fed myself spiritually." And doing these changes everything.

Total immersion is a lifestyle.
No more "Sunday Christian" and "part-time Christianity."
It's full-time, 24/7, lay-it-all-down, Jesus-is-everything Christianity.

No Time to Waste / Patient Endurance

I know every generation says, *"This is the generation Jesus is coming back,"* but in 2025, I cannot express just how much I believe that this is truly the time. Prophecies are being fulfilled, signs and wonders are manifesting, and prodigals are returning home. It's just like Jesus said: *"As it was in the days of Noah..."* The world is in complete chaos. But we as believers walk in an unshakable inner peace, knowing we're already standing on the victory side. We know how the story ends, and because we know, there's an urgency burning within us to make heaven crowded by sharing the gospel of salvation to everyone. To shout from the rooftops that the enemy really does come to steal, kill, and destroy, and that only God can bring life - and life more abundantly.

I spent so long on the wrong team. I was on the team that steals, kills, and destroys. But now I'm on God's team! It's the greatest gift I've ever known. It's the greatest peace in the middle of chaos, and the greatest joy in the middle of sorrow. Everything I was ever looking for - I found in Him.

I wonder how many people are just like I was. I was merely a confessing Christian. Before my salvation in 2016, I truly thought that if I had died, I was going to heaven simply because I believed in Jesus. But that's not what the Bible says. The Bible says, *"You must be born again."* And I absolutely was not born again.

My husband and I were on "The All-Jesus Podcast" recently, with our friend and host, Pete Cabrera Jr. - I was asked this question: *"What was the sign that you weren't really a Christian?"* And I knew the answer instantly. It was my ability to actively sin - to lie, to cheat, and to manipulate without batting an eye. I could call myself a Christian but continue to do things that were against God without feeling guilt or shame. I wore a mask pretending to be a good person, but I was sold out to the world. My heart belonged to the enemy.

I remember hearing Todd White once say that his mission is to lead Christians to Christ. That was me - a confessing Christian who didn't allow Jesus to be Lord of their life. I had not been born again.

Is that you?
Can you willfully and actively sin?
Can you do whatever you want without feeling conviction?
Do you believe, like I once did, that God is like Santa Claus - that all you have to do is believe that He exists and you'll get a present?

Well, guess what?
It's not true. You're either on the enemy's team or you're on God's team. So, if you're reading this book and you're not sure whether you're going to heaven or not - you can make the decision to know for sure right now!

Like my husband always says when he's out evangelizing:

"Are you going to heaven with me?" If Jesus were to come back in the next two hours - would you be ready?

I want you to know that there's no time to waste. You can ask Jesus to be Lord of your life today. If you've never done this before, here is the easiest way to remember the ABC's of salvation:

A=Admit. B=Believe. C=Confess.

But it's got to be more than just repeating a prayer.

It's got to be a decision. It's got to be a lifestyle change. It's got to be you saying:

> *"Jesus, I want You to come in and help me make these changes. I don't want to be the person I am today. I want to be different. And I know that only You can do that work in me. So I make a conscious decision to play on Your team and no longer play for the world. I believe in you. Come into my life, wash me clean, and become the Lord of my life. Amen."*

Believers vs. Disciples

A believer is someone who holds a belief in God.
A disciple is someone who actively follows and imitates the teachings of God.

I used to think God was like Santa Claus, and just like they tell you at Christmas - *"All you have to do is believe, and you get a gift."* I had the perspective that if I just believed in God, I got into heaven. But that's not what the Bible says.

When Nicodemus asked Jesus, *"How do you get into the kingdom of heaven?"* Jesus told him, *"You must be born again."* Now looking back, I know that I wasn't born again. We're all born into sin, but until we are born again, we haven't died with Christ or risen with Him. That means we haven't been made new. I think so many people give God lip service. They play the part of being a confessing Christian, but Jesus isn't Lord of their life. They don't honor Him, they don't love Him, they don't obey His commandments, they don't spend time with Him, and they don't read His Word to find out His direction.

I remember once, I was in a study group with some new believers, trying to explain this exact thing. And I asked if they remembered the movie *Training Day* with Denzel Washington? He played a corrupt cop in a drug infested neighborhood. Police officers are supposed to defend justice and uphold the law, but that's not at all what his character did. He was a thief, a liar, and a manipulator.

I think so many of us are like that - corrupt Christians. We say one thing and do another. That's hypocrisy, and it's such a bad representation of Jesus Christ to the lost.

I knew what it was like to live like the world.
So, when I got saved in 2016, I wanted to live fully for God. I was all in and completely sold out for Jesus with everything that it entailed. Honestly, I just began doing the opposite of what I had done before. I changed from making bad choices to making good choices. Old Kim lied and manipulated. New and born-again Kim walks in integrity and tells the truth - no matter what the cost. Old Kim could lie and steal without blinking an eye, but now, conviction and love have changed my heart. I don't want to do those things. I had never been faithful in a physical relationship with men, and with God, it was no different.
I would tell Him I loved Him, and I would sing Him songs, but my life and my choices did not match my words. I know now that being a disciple means I give up my thoughts, my plans, and what I think is right - and I surrender to what God wants and submit to His will.

It's like Mr. Miyagi and his student from the movie "Karate Kid". The relationship they had was one where his student Daniel trusted that Mr. Miyagi had all the wisdom. Even when it didn't make sense, he trusted that Miyagi knew what he was doing. Sometimes, it's just like that with God. Sometimes, we're doing a "wax on, wax off" exercise that makes no sense in the natural, but God is truly the Potter, and we are the clay. If we allow Him to have full control, His plans for us are perfect. He's a good Father. He doesn't withhold any good things. The best decision I ever made was to shut off my brain and quit trying to figure everything out. I finally let the Holy Spirit, God the Father, and Jesus the Healer be the answer. And if I didn't know the immediate answer, I would search it out. I would find it in His Word. Everything we could ever ask for and need is right there in His Word. But more importantly - you must spend time with Him. You have to sit with Him, rest in His goodness, and listen to His direction. You have to be intentional about getting to know Him, just like you would be in a relationship with a boyfriend, girlfriend, or spouse.

A believer goes to church to check it off their weekly list. A disciple goes to church to do the Word of God, because they know: Faith comes by hearing.

A believer is led by their feelings, emotions, unforgiveness, and offense, and rarely minding the Word of God. But a disciple knows we're not led by emotions. We're not led by feelings. The Word of God is first place and final authority.

A believer is accountable to no one.
A disciple is accountable to everyone.

A disciple knows their witness is their greatest gift. When they are squeezed, what flows out should be the fruit of the Spirit, not anger.

A believer seeks God only when there's a crisis.
And when the storm passes? They stop. They walk away.
But a disciple? A disciple never stops seeking. They pursue God every moment, every hour, and every second of the

day - for instruction, guidance, and correction. A believer has to be told they are wrong.

But a disciple? A disciple welcomes correction, because they know - Growth is the greatest gift.

So I ask you... Which are you?
Are you just giving God *lip service*?
Are you letting the empty wells the world offers control your life? Are you running to sex, drugs, or alcohol to satisfy you?

At the end of the day, what do you turn to when you're happy? What do you turn to when you're sad?

How would you describe your life right now?

Do you run to the world?
Or do you run to God?

Do you want to know how I got from dope to hope?

"I went from being a believer to being a disciple.
I stopped giving God lip service, and I truly let Him be Lord of my life. I got out of the driver's seat and turned over my keys to my Creator."

And you can too.

Dedication

To my forever supportive husband, Armando Perez - the man I waited four and a half years for... but somehow knew my entire life. The man God created just for me.
As my sweet mother-in-law says, *"my Twinkie."*

To my children - Cameron, Paige, Noah, and Drake - Thank you for your unconditional love and unwavering support. You are my greatest blessings.

To my mom, my number one fan and fiercest prayer warrior, and to Pop Pop, for his generous heart, his willingness to feed others with love, and for showing compassion in everything he does.

To my dad, who faithfully trained up his children in the Lord and has always been there when we need him.

To my War Rooms Nation Tent Team, you are more than a ministry team. You are family.

And to my siblings, you are loved!

A special 'Thank You" to every single one of you who gave so generously to help make this vision a reality:

- **Melissa Lang**
- **Taytum Mendes**
- **Sarah Lytle**
- **Deana Bruno**
- **Christina Foster** (Sis)
- **Ed Kopal** (Dad)
- **Kathy Matlock** (Mom)
- **Audra Littou**
- **Crystal Morales**
- **Jennifer Palmer**
- **Lupe Juarez**
- **Linda Herrera**

Thank you.
Your love, your support, and your faith in this journey mean more than words could ever say.

Thank you for reading this book. Let us know about the decision you made and how this book has impacted you. We are rejoicing with you!

Armando & Kim Perez
Contact: aperezbooks@outlook.com

Cover layout by Jenn Foster - eliteonlinepublishing.com
Written by Kim Kopal Perez